To learn more about the Micro Focus Operations Bridge, our Hybrid IT monitoring solution, visit http://microfocus.com/opsbridge.

Connect with us on Twitter, @MicroFocusITOps, or our blog at http://tiny.cc/opsbridge-blog.

You can also see videos of what customers have to say at http://tiny.cc/opsbridge-youtube.

Next Generation IT Operations

Automated Hybrid IT Operations Management

How will you transform your operations management?

Ian Bromehead, Wes Cooper, Michael Procopio

THiNKaha®

E-mail: info@thinkaha.com
20660 Stevens Creek Blvd., Suite 210
Cupertino, CA 95014

⇨ Please go to http://aha.pub/HybridITOps to read this AHAbook and to share the individual AHAmessages that resonate with you.

Published by THiNKaha®
20660 Stevens Creek Blvd., Suite 210, Cupertino, CA 95014
http://thinkaha.com
E-mail: info@thinkaha.com

First Printing: January 2019
Second Printing: March 2019
Hardcover ISBN: 978-1-61699-314-6 1-61699-314-6
Paperback ISBN: 978-1-61699-313-9 1-61699-313-8
eBook ISBN: 978-1-61699-312-2 1-61699-312-X
Place of Publication: Silicon Valley, California, USA
Paperback Library of Congress Number: 2018967994

How to Read a THiNKaha® Book

A Note from the Publisher

The AHAthat/THiNKaha series is the CliffsNotes of the 21st century. These books are contextual in nature. Although the actual words won't change, their meaning will every time you read one as your context will change. Be ready, you will experience your own AHA moments as you read the AHA messages™ in this book. They are designed to be stand-alone actionable messages that will help you think about a project you're working on, an event, a sales deal, a personal issue, etc. differently. As you read this book, please think about the following:

1. It should only take 15–20 minutes to read this book the first time out. When you're reading, write in the underlined area one to three action items that resonate with you.
2. Mark your calendar to re-read this book again in 30 days.
3. Repeat step #1 and mark one to three more AHA messages that resonate. They will most likely be different than the first time. BTW: this is also a great time to reflect on the AHA messages that resonated with you during your last reading.

After reading a THiNKaha book, marking your AHA messages, re-reading it, and marking more AHA messages, you'll begin to see how these books contextually apply to you. AHAthat/THiNKaha books advocate for continuous, lifelong learning. They will help you transform your AHAs into actionable items with tangible results until you no longer have to say AHA to these moments—they'll become part of your daily practice as you continue to grow and learn.

Mitchell Levy, The AHA Guy at AHAthat
publisher@thinkaha.com

THiNKaha®

Contents

Foreword by Luke Bradley

Ours is a digital company, and the corporate culture focuses on ensuring a competitive edge with user experience and predictable service quality at its core. Pragmatically, nothing must stop the business functioning; service has to be excellent, simple, and at everyone's fingertips.

Increasingly centralized and hyperscale services means that the reputation of the brand can be impacted so quickly and easily. A major outage or security incident can have the reputational impact similar to that of a catastrophic event in the Airline and Nuclear Power industry. There is minimal margin for error, and the priority has to be on zero downtime.

From an IT operations perspective, that means that we must have forensic visibility across the board. We have to see the health of all dependent resources and services. Our daily lives are evolving quickly, however, and the leaps and bounds in open technologies have resulted in technologies such as containers, cloud, mobile apps, Kafka, and Kubernetes being increasingly present in our IT landscape.

Clearly now, IT processes, tools, and skills simply have to evolve to embrace all these. The cultural transformation associated with DevOps is seen as a critical component to supporting these many shifts in the industry. But no one can afford to scrap legacy resources. So, when managing a high frequency of change that is needed in modern apps in order to stay competitive, we're heavily constrained due to these older resources. Coordination across multiple elements, multiple business units, can be a real challenge and barrier to evolution.

Operationally, realizing the promise of DevOps is only pragmatically doable at a relatively limited scale, partially because of such constraints. The hunt for DevOps at the enterprise scale is on, but obtaining the promised gains will mean adopting elements of ITOM during the conception of the application. Taking Monitoring as an example, we see full service instrumentation generating enormous volumes of data, so centralizing it and applying automated analytics is a must. So, too, is doing machine learning on the fly, but it comes with its own challenges. For example, how can machine learning be effective to help operations if you are making frequent releases to your application and there isn't a real baseline of what good looks like?

Much like the Airline or Nuclear Power industry, forensically being able to understand why an outage happened will be critical to understanding Root Cause and making sure that the outage won't be repeated. A Reliability Engineering approach will increase the probability that Continuous Improvement will ensure that we are pro-actively managing alignment to objectives of the business. Parallels between those processes and ITIL are immediately apparent.

Such a close collaboration between the Business, Development, and Ops will make it virtually impossible to separate the Business from Technology. DevOps will become BizOps, whereby the Business will see ITOM requirements as the critical components of their service. Automation, Data, Machine Learning, self-healing systems, these are all domains that define evolution to our next generation operations management, and open tools have a vital role to play if we are to achieve BizOps at scale in a modern and scaled enterprise.

Luke Bradley
Senior Manager of Engineering
Operations Engineering & Transformation
Technology Shared Services (TSS)
Vodafone Group Services Limited

Foreword by Toine Jenniskens

When I get asked what the future of IT Operations Management (ITOM) is, the first thing that pops into mind is: Is there ITOM in the future? There are trends like DevOps, Artificial Intelligence, No-Ops, Automation, Cloud, etc. They all promise less cost and Faster Time to Value. So, is there ITOM in this future? Or do you still need ITOM when you get there?

I sincerely think you do. ITOM will change but you still need it. Would you want to drive a car without some metrics and sense of direction presented to you on your dashboard? Even if it is a Tesla or some other self-driving car? Do you TRUST the technology enough?

I think it is fair to say that in general, we don't trust our cars enough to skip measuring its quality and having some kind of control over it. The same goes for IT, at least for the next decade. After that, maybe the robots take over. ;-)

But as I mentioned, sure, ITOM will change, and that is where the trends come in. When you move more and more to the cloud, you yourself don't have to measure everything in depth. You measure the Contract you agreed on with the provider. The provider does the rest of the ITOM (IT doesn't go away). Also, DevOps will change ITOM in the way that, across Development and Operations, backlogs are slowly but surely merging, and ITOM (Quality and Management) is more and more a topic, from the conception of a new application to the decommissioning of it.

Also, ITOM is automating fast, and Artificial Intelligence will even increase this with Self Learning ITOM, automated remediation of incidents. Analytics will improve monitoring, which will get us better delivery of our apps. Less outage, better performance, and less or better mitigated risk. Because IT is getting too complex for humans to grasp, and because Automation will prove to make fewer mistakes.

So, if you are reading or browsing through this book, you will find that it provides some views on what I also see happening around me and what I believe the future will bring. Whether it is by the introduction of new technologies, Automation, more and/or other data, and different IT delivery models like Cloud, you have to get ready for it! You have to start automating your event management, build your intelligence to catch the anomalies early, and automate your incident response, or better yet, automate everything! The trends will not wait for you to pick up. ;-)

IT will still have to be managed somehow by someone, so: Be sure that there is still a bright and interesting future for ITOM, but act now!

Toine Jenniskens
Business Architect
Rabobank

Foreword by Travis Greene

In the 1920s, the lifespan of an S&P 500 company was sixty-seven years. Today, it is fifteen. Disruption is being led by those companies that are able to innovate digitally. Eighty-seven percent of CEOs say they are in the innovation business, but IT budgets show something different. Only 16 percent is spent on innovation. The vast majority of IT budget allocation—averaging over 80 percent—is spent on running IT operations and making incremental changes.

The result is that more and more of the IT Operations budget is moving to cloud-based providers of infrastructure and applications. Just a few years ago, enterprises were generally cloud-averse. Today, companies say that 68 percent of new deployments will be off-premises by 2020. But with cloud being common, it loses its innovative benefits relative to competitors. If you're building apps to increase your differentiation from competitors, how can a shared cloud app deliver that differentiation?

A new wave of disruptive technology is therefore emerging. Technology-leading enterprises are deploying containers to offer more flexible deployment options to fulfill the insatiable demand for rapid DevOps infrastructure provisioning.

This is an opportunity for IT Operations because containers are going to be deployed in multiple clouds and on-premises. Without a single cloud provider, enterprises need a central organization to consistently manage performance and delivery of services in a secure and compliant manner. Rather than accepting a position as curators of legacy environments, IT Operations must re-assert its necessary roles of service management, fulfillment, assurance, and governance with a foundation of analytics and AIOps to help you gain insights and respond in real time. Doing this correctly will accelerate DevOps practices and deliver business insights for greater innovation, without sacrificing security, risk, and governance.

To accomplish this transformation, IT Operations management needs to evolve toward Hybrid IT Management. Container and cloud-based solutions have their place, but systems and services with decades of investment cannot be replaced overnight without significant cost and risk. Hybrid IT Management is a flexible approach that unifies IT Operations across both traditional and transformational infrastructure and applications, so you can achieve the balance of both running and transforming your business.

The speed, scale, and complexity of hybrid environments cannot be addressed without analytics and automation. Insight is needed in time to act, and automation will reduce the reaction time to avoid business disruption. Hybrid IT Management demands an AIOps foundation.

In *Next Generation IT Operations*, you'll find thought-provoking and inspirational nuggets that are quick and useful for your journey to transform your operations to Hybrid IT Management. Because the business has to keep running while we transform.

Good luck on your journey.

Travis Greene
Sr. Director of Product Marketing, Micro Focus
IT Operations Management

Introduction

Is monitoring boring?

Some, maybe many, will say yes. However, enterprise architectures are always evolving, so the process of performance monitoring, data collection, and data exploitation needs to evolve congruently.

Managing IT Operations at the speed of DevOps is a tough ambition, but it's the target that IT must shoot for if they want to inspire real transformation and deliver value to the business.

We have observed that many IT operations teams are understaffed and that the number of skilled people is not increasing, but decreasing. So, how do IT operations teams transform to embrace the newer technologies included in modern application architectures? How do they embed their skills and experience into today's business requirements, given these restraints?

After watching recordings of specialists presenting at AWS conferences and preaching monitoring-as-code, we wondered how people not experienced in operations could be expected to define instrumentation. How would they know which log entries to write, how often, and with what level of information?

If developers aren't involved much in deploying, then how would they know what level of documentation is needed to ensure correct deployment and to allow operations to determine when anomalies are happening?

Surely, increased information sharing and collaboration must happen as per a real DevOps definition. Becoming pragmatic is accelerated by having the right tools and processes to foster strong collaboration.

Typically, we're almost forced into a constant context of varying degrees of compromise. No application developer can claim to be a master at operations, and no operator is a master at creating effective applications. Such skills aren't abundant, and the respective constraints and measures around their roles don't give them liberty to extend much beyond their immediate daily lives.

Tools can help.

Tools can embed skills that are missing or aren't regularly available when most needed. They can automate tasks that are otherwise time consuming, and help negate the need for situation or war rooms. Does anyone have time for those, anyway?

We all know how easy it is to make mistakes through distraction or tiredness. Automation can relieve the situation, consistently executing common laborious tasks.

Couple both analytics and automation, and it's easy to see just how desirable such tools can become.

While Gartner has detailed recommendations concerning analytics or artificial intelligence applied to operations (AIOps), they don't include nearly enough articulation of the need to *automate* AIOps. Who has enough staff to manually apply all the recommendations they make to all data types you can gather with monitoring? Automated AIOps makes powerful algorithmic-driven monitoring more valuable. It delivers autonomous actions to ride tandem with manual operators and maintain high quality of service.

We hope that these pages will inspire your thoughts and lead your research around defining your priorities for next-generation operations management.

Ian, Michael, and Wes

IT professionals can now be strategic business partners by providing actionable insights to their stakeholders' data, allowing them to make more effective decisions faster. #HybridIT

http://aha.pub/HybridITOps

Share the AHA messages from this book socially by going to http://aha.pub/HybridITOps

Section I

The Changing Role of IT and Business

Times are changing. Businesses need to keep up with the fast-paced growth of technology in today's world. Application providers must consistently give the level of service their users expect from them. If your service is slow, users can simply go to a different site. The end users' experience is critical to be competitive and stay in business.

1

IT professionals are becoming more business literate and business professionals more IT literate, so together, they can collaborate to more effectively compete and service customers. #HybridIT

2

Skilled and experienced IT professionals are now seen as valuable and strategic business partners and are less likely to be outsourced. #HybridIT

3

IT professionals can now be strategic business partners by providing actionable data and insight to their stakeholders in terms that allow them to make more effective decisions faster. #HybridIT

4

IT operations teams can transform to help businesses be a more capable service provider that's more than just keeping servers alive. #HybridIT

5

Businesses must exploit IT's capability to measure and impact the quality of service that customers consume online. #HybridIT

6

A modern business-oriented IT department must be able to see how a resource affects a business service — that means understanding dependencies. #HybridIT

7

#HybridITmanagement is changing how IT and business work together to serve customers by providing better and more efficient monitoring, analysis, and automation. #HybridIT

8

Enterprise #HybridITmanagement solutions scale to show their entire operation on a single screen vs. wasting time scanning multiple screens and data sources to understand the situation. #HybridIT

9

#HybridITmanagement solutions help identify which alerts from which resources impact business users or targets and which to ignore. #HybridIT

10

#HybridITmanagement solutions provide businesses with increased agility and cost management, and a dashboard to monitor it all. #HybridIT

11

IT Operations must move from an infrastructure provider to a service broker. #HybridIT

Share the AHA messages from this book socially by going to
http://aha.pub/HybridITOps

Section II

Moving to Cloud and Managing Multiple Vendors

Nowadays, most businesses are using multiple cloud vendors, which is why finding and fixing problems is harder than ever. Cloud vendors provide monitoring services, but only for their own cloud. This makes it difficult to get an end-to-end view without using a hybrid IT management solution.

With the help of hybrid IT management solutions, businesses can now see the data from all their cloud vendors and on-premise systems in a single screen, thus enabling them to be more efficient in serving their customers.

12

Don't put things into the cloud without measuring. How can you manage a situation you're not monitoring? #HybridIT

13

The more cloud tools you have, the harder it is to visualize how your business is doing. #HybridITmanagement solutions show the complete picture and guide you to improve. #HybridIT

14

Without visibility over how applications behave in the cloud, you won't see how much a service incident costs. #HybridITmanagement prevents incidents and reduces costs. #HybridIT

15

Businesses using multi-cloud need better monitoring capabilities than those provided by their cloud vendors. #HybridIT

16

If your service goes down, the user doesn't care whether it's you or the cloud provider at fault. You're the person who promised to give them service. #HybridITmanagement helps you keep your promises. #HybridIT

17

Having a tool from each cloud vendor and one for on-premise causes too much noise. #HybridITmanagement solutions reduce and show data in a single console, allowing your operators to see the signal through the noise. #HybridIT

18

Disparate, non-integrated cloud tools don't allow for an end-to-end view. Integration gives you a cleaner perspective of what's going on. #HybridIT

19

#HybridITmanagement solutions can detect cloud disruptions fast to allow you to quickly apply contingencies and prevent long outages. #HybridIT

20

When using multiple cloud vendors, you need new monitoring solutions to centralize the alerts from all cloud vendors. #HybridIT

21

#HybridITmanagement solutions compile and analyze data from multiple cloud vendors to isolate problems and qualify their impact. #HybridIT

22

#HybridITmanagement solutions show you what's happening and in which cloud as it happens. #HybridIT

23

Monitoring your #HybridCloud infrastructure provides visibility over the health of applications and resources used by businesses to achieve better service delivery. #HybridIT

24

When you put apps in the cloud, you need #HybridITmanagement solutions to detect abnormalities faster. #HybridIT

25

Forward-thinking businesses that use multiple cloud monitoring tools purchase #HybridITmanagement solutions to better monitor all their data. How many cloud tools are you using? #HybridIT

26

Do you want to know what's happening with your cloud services in real time? A business value dashboard can show services across multiple cloud and on-premise systems. #HybridIT

27

A business value dashboard lets you see your cloud costs and visually correlate for capacity planning. #HybridIT

28

The longer it takes to find which cloud a problem is in means a longer outage that costs more. How long does it take you to find the source of your problems? #HybridIT

Share the AHA messages from this book socially by going to http://aha.pub/HybridITOps

Section III

Ensuring Ongoing Security and Compliance

Moving to the cloud comes with certain risks, specifically security and compliance issues. Application providers need to ensure that their systems are secure and compliant to the business's regulations to avoid major outages that could affect the service they provide to their users.

29

The nature of the cloud means an increase in issues from a general security, compliance, and data security perspective. How secure are you? #HybridIT

30

Organizations need to control compliance and find issues previously unencountered, often due to someone somewhere making mistakes. #HybridITmanagement helps! #HybridIT

31

Do you have security and compliancy concerns deploying new applications using the cloud? #HybridITmanagement solutions can show you if and where there's a weak link. #HybridIT

32

#HybridITmanagement solutions detect authentication and hacker issues, which can cause service disruptions. Can you find and fix them fast enough? #HybridIT

33

#HybridITmanagement solutions capture configuration changes accurately so you can see if there's a compliance violation or if it wasn't set up properly. #HybridIT

34

#HybridITmanagement solutions can rewind a configuration error to go back to the situation before the error occurred. #HybridIT

35

#HybridIT management solutions use analytics to find configurations that might be a compliance violation. #HybridIT

36

Before restarting a server, store the logs and info that will help you understand why a compliance or security problem occurred in the first place. #HybridIT

37

Apply analytics to find out what the security hazards are so you can prioritize what you're going to do first. #HybridIT

38

How fast are you capable of detecting a hacking violation when someone is trying to break into your authentication system? #HybridIT

39

If your security people detect a security hazard but don't have the info of which systems are going to be impacted, they only have a partial picture of what's going on and won't be able to act as quickly. #HybridIT

40

With a #HybridITmanagement solution, you'll have a complete picture of the security hazard happening in your business to help you figure out what to do next. #HybridIT

41

Security issues, which can constitute a risk of $50 million of business per minute, can greatly impact your organization. Can your monitoring detect these issues? #HybridIT

42

Your IT people have to maintain compliant systems by upgrading and installing patches required to keep them secure. #HybridITmanagement helps! #HybridIT

43

#HybridITmanagement solutions help you ensure that you are deploying configurations in line with compliance directives. #HybridIT

44

Automated compliance helps businesses help themselves to be more secure in rolling out new capabilities aimed to serve customers better. Are you using automated compliance? #HybridIT

45

#HybridITmanagement solutions provide automated compliance and forced implementation, which helps business work more efficiently. #HybridIT

Share the AHA messages from this book socially by going to http://aha.pub/HybridITOps

Section IV

Monitoring, Dashboards, and Reporting

IT operations is now in a new, faster-paced world. Hybrid IT, DevOps, Shadow IT, the volume of data generated, end user experience sensitivity, and budget reductions keep IT Operations teams under more pressure than ever to deliver.

To ease that pressure, automated hybrid IT management solutions provide businesses with an easier way to automatically discover and monitor resources as they come online, as well as provide dashboards and reports, to focus on business impact.

46

You can't manage what you can't measure. Monitoring collects data, dashboards provide real-time actionable insights in an easily consumable form, and reporting provides a look backward and forward. #HybridIT

47

Do you spend hours with people arguing about what the problem was, why the outage occurred, and how you could have avoided it, and not ever getting to the root cause? #HybridIT

48

Tools integration can help operators work on the root cause of problems quickly and efficiently. Are your tools integrated? #HybridIT

49

#HybridITmanagement solutions integrate the data from multiple tools so you can qualify problems in one place. #HybridIT

50

If your services are down, how much does it cost you? #HybridITmanagement helps you prevent outages. #ITOps #HybridIT

___

___

___

51

You must identify the trends moving toward potential disasters fast enough to find and fix them before they impact your business. #HybridIT

52

Disparate, non-integrated tools present too much info. #HybridITmanagement integration provides focus and a cleaner perspective of what's going on in your business. #HybridIT

53

If most of your operators are always in firefighting mode, how will you shift them to operate new architectures using #HybridIT?

54

Do you have the right toolset to be able to capture the right info and see what's impacting your business? #HybridIT

55

How can you handle multiple events simultaneously if you have 15 consoles in front of you? You'll be forever lagging behind what's happening in real time. #HybridITmanagement helps. #HybridIT

56

High operations cost is what people want to get rid of. Every problem ticket you open incurs costs. #HybridITmanagement solutions help reduce incidents/tickets. How much are you spending on tickets? #HybridIT

57

How often do you have outages? How much time do you spend looking for the root cause of the outage? #HybridIT

58

Can't see how you're consuming the resources you're paying for? #HybridITmanagement solutions help you understand your business operations better. #HybridIT

59

#HybridITmanagement solutions help you monitor what you have within your own entity and integrate the data from multiple applications. #HybridIT

60

Anything that can impact the end-to-end performance of your services needs to be captured and monitored. You can't manage what you don't measure. #HybridIT

61

Cloud vendors can generate so many alerts, you're just staring at a sea of red. #HybridITmanagement solutions can filter and prioritize alerts. #HybridIT

62

#HybridITmanagement solutions give you a proper handle on how many of your services are being consumed by your customers and whether they're performing adequately. #HybridIT

63

One way that #HybridITmanagement solutions help businesses understand what's happening during a major application outage is by capturing and documenting the problem. #HybridIT

64

With the right #HybridITmanagement solution, your operations team won't need to be in firefighting and reactive mode all the time because they'll have the information to deal with the situation. #HybridIT

65

#HybridITmanagement solutions quickly measure and capture bad trends that are making your connectivity worse or completely breaking it. #HybridIT

66

#HybridITmanagement solutions capture outages that are happening in your business so you can find a way to avoid them. Are you capturing outages? #HybridIT

67

#HybridITmanagement solutions let you know how many users you have, where those users are, and if they are satisfied. #HybridIT

68

#HybridITmanagement solutions monitor everything in your business to help you understand how situations arise and which one is impacting the business the most, so you can then act to remove the problem. #HybridIT

69

Do you want to know what's happening with your business services in real time? A business value dashboard is live news for IT. #HybridIT

70

A business value dashboard illustrates IT and business data clearly on your device of choice, whether that's a mobile phone, tablet, or virtually any device with a browser. Do you have a business value dashboard? #HybridIT

71

Before restarting a server, store the logs and info that will help you understand why the problem occurred in the first place. #HybridIT

72

Remedial action should be more intelligent than just simply restarting servers. It should help us understand the corrective action. #HybridIT

73

#HybridITmanagement solutions let you know if and when something is disrupting your business and whose fault it is. Know where your weak link is and how you can use automated remediation to solve it. #HybridIT

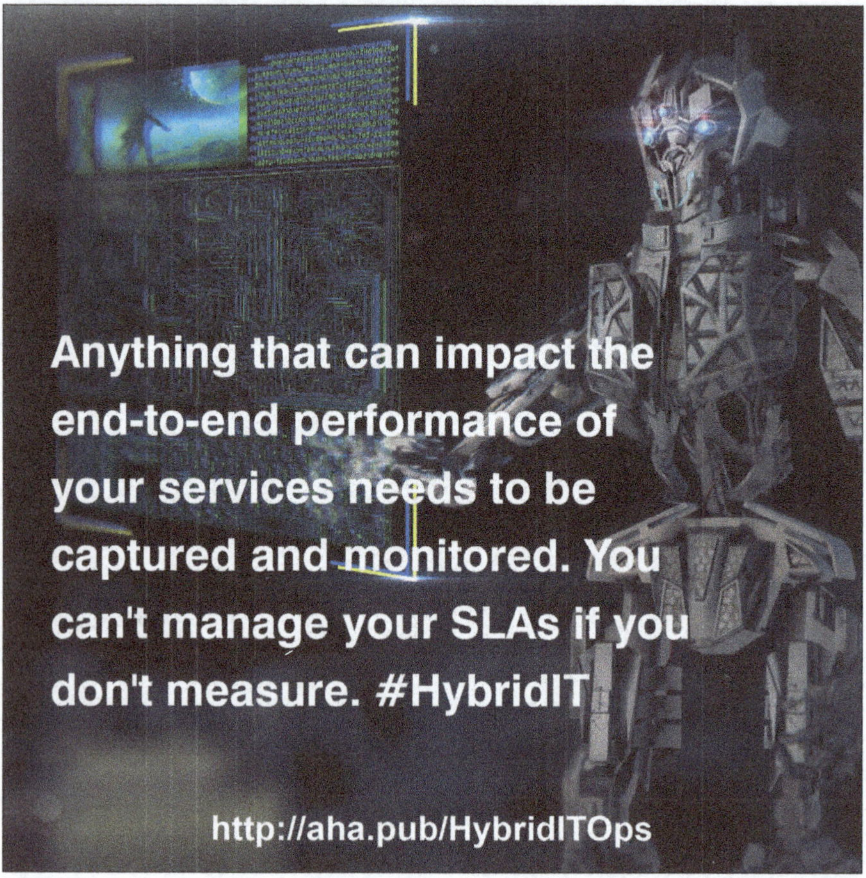

Share the AHA messages from this book socially by going to http://aha.pub/HybridITOps

Section V

Automated AIOps and Remediation

Today's Operations teams have to deal with massive volumes of metrics, events, logs, and topology/dependency data, more than any human can consume. This is why Artificial Intelligence IT Operations (AIOps) is so important.

Automation provides a virtual workforce to keep your systems alive and fix them when a problem comes up. AI provides insights from the massive data collected and can guide the automation. Used together, you become more agile and compete faster and better.

74

Automated AIOps is the use of artificial intelligence and automation in the practice of IT Operations. #HybridIT

75

Analytics help you understand where new problems are occurring and why. #HybridIT

76

#HybridITmanagement solutions help you implement best practices that your users can use, activate, and execute automatically to solve issues. What are your best practices? #HybridIT

77

Automation is important because today, resources come and go but still need to be managed. #HybridIT

78

Automated self-learning, qualification, root cause, cost analysis, and remediation reduce operational costs. Can your tools apply automation? #HybridIT

79

Metrics, events, logs, and topology/ dependency data are massive, more than any human can consume. Automated monitoring solutions help you handle those massive amounts of data. #HybridIT

80

#HybridITmanagement solutions give people access to all the data you have in one place so it's easier for you to let people analyze and extract info for their own interests. #HybridIT

81

Analytics surfaces data to help operators who don't have the right skills find problems faster. #HybridIT

82

If you don't have robotics and automation, you won't be able to handle the number of events you're facing. Automate! #HybridIT

83

Automate best practices to solve a problem, so your users can consume your services faster than contacting customer service. #HybridIT

84

Automate the process of making sure that your monitoring data is defined for all your resources and that monitoring can bring info back to where you need it. #HybridIT

85

Automation allows less skilled operators to fix issues in minutes that they otherwise would have to escalate to more expensive personnel. #HybridIT

86

Artificial intelligence acts on its findings to either propose an action to an operator or activate automation to perform an action for an operator to quickly resolve a problem. #HybridIT

87

When your operators can't react fast enough to resolve problems, you'll need to integrate and automate your tools and processes. #HybridIT

88

With automation, you can repurpose your people's skills to do more important things that can help the business grow even further. #HybridIT

89

Finding the root cause out of all the info that comes to your screens takes skill and time. How do you handle the absurd amount of data? #HybridITmanagement helps! #HybridIT

90

Good visibility enables you to predict and measure the cost of issues quickly and to prevent them from happening again. #HybridIT

91

Automation provides you a virtual workforce to keep your systems alive and healthy to become more agile and compete faster and better. #HybridIT

92

Robotic Process Automation (#RPA) with artificial intelligence can automatically find and fix problems like a human. In its infancy now, but watch it grow! #HybridIT

Share the AHA messages from this book socially by going to
http://aha.pub/HybridITOps

Section VI

Ensuring Service-Level Agreements

Application providers strive to maintain a high quality of service to their users. If their service fails to meet the expectations of their customers, either they get penalized or their users look for service someplace else.

Ensuring that application providers deliver their service-level agreements to customers is crucial to staying in business.

93

Measure yourself to see if you're providing what you promised to your customers. Are you keeping your SLAs? #HybridIT

94

Without monitoring your applications from a user perspective, you may never know that you're losing business because you're not providing good service. #HybridIT

95

How much does it cost you if your services are down? It's typically tens of thousands of dollars. #HybridITmanagement helps you prevent and fix outages. #HybridIT

96

Automate the process of making sure your monitoring data is assigned to all your resources and that monitoring can bring SLA info back to where you need it. #HybridIT

97

Anything that can impact the end-to-end performance of your services needs to be captured and monitored. You can't manage your SLAs if you don't measure. #HybridIT

98

Set up service objectives to protect your brand. Monitoring can help you detect and manage a situation that can degrade your brand. Are you monitoring? #HybridIT

____

____

____

99

IT executives use SLA metrics to measure their staff. #HybridITmanagement solutions help staff attain those metrics. #HybridIT

100

A service-level agreement (SLA) is a contractual relationship between a business and its customers to deliver the quality of service defined by specified metrics. #HybridIT

101

Monitoring SLAs is important; it detects when you're getting close to breaching your promises to your customers. #HybridIT

102

Non-contractual SLOs can be measured by the level of satisfaction of your customers, your actual response time, and service performance. Do you have SLOs? #HybridIT

103

Service level objectives (SLOs) are more internal than SLAs, which are written and signed between two different parties. #HybridIT

104

As you get closer to breaching your SLOs or SLAs, you need to more closely watch your monitored data and be ready to increase resources. #HybridIT

105

How many days/weeks/months is your IT team capable of maintaining your SLAs? #HybridITmanagement solutions can give them the boost they need. #HybridIT

106

When a customer is purchasing a book with a credit card and the system suddenly freezes, #HybridITmanagement solutions can provide the reason. #HybridIT

107

#HybridITmanagement solutions provide you with a backup of your important diagnostic data, without needing to contact the help desk. #HybridIT

108

Respect your SLAs and SLOs to make sure you're managing and governing your service delivery properly so you can satisfy customers and protect your brand. #HybridIT

109

Businesses employ IT professionals to ensure that systems don't go down, and if they do, they can switch to an alternative system quickly, maintaining SLAs. #HybridIT

110

Switching to a different data center after the primary crashes can still disrupt SLAs due to the extra load on the backup center. #HybridITmanagement solutions help you avoid overloading your data center. #HybridIT

111

#HybridITmanagement solutions help you prevent degrading your service levels when outages occur. #HybridIT

112

Are you responsible for the quality of service that's being delivered to your users? #HybridITmanagement helps you keep your SLAs. #HybridIT

______

______

______

113

Without visibility during a service outage, you won't be able to respond quickly. People won't do business with you and will go elsewhere. #HybridITmanagement helps. #HybridIT

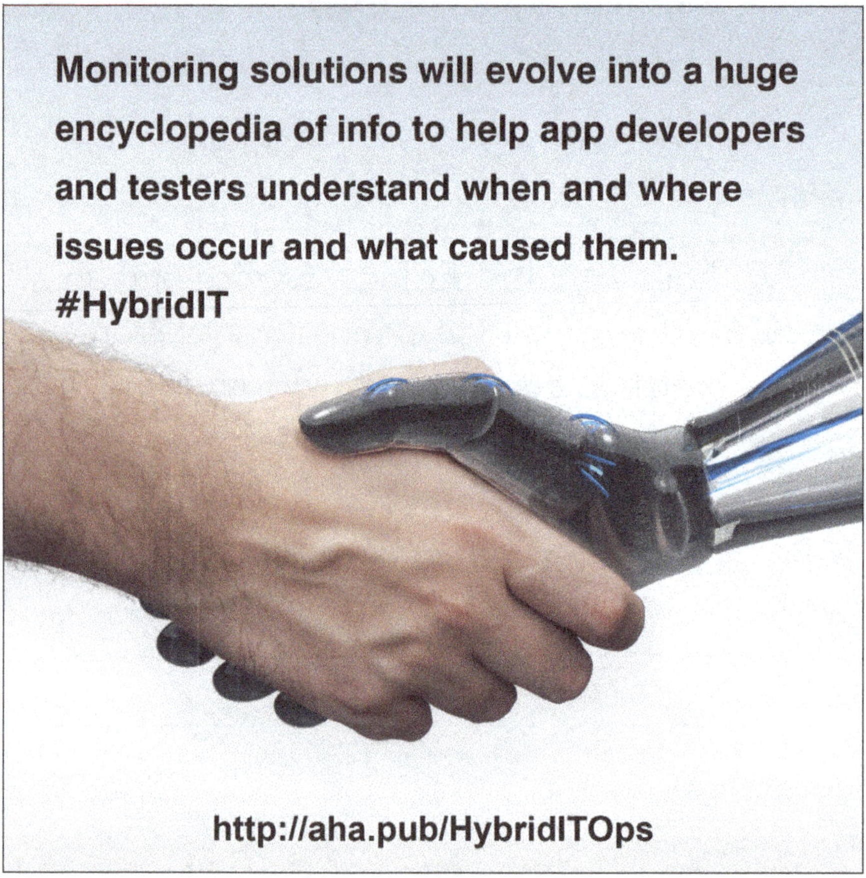

Share the AHA messages from this book socially by going to http://aha.pub/HybridITOps

Section VII

The Future of IT Operations

Going forward, we will see the acceleration of recent trends and new ways of delivering service. Containers, DevOps, SecOps, NetSecOps, service-defined everything, and service brokering are just a few things IT Operations will have to embrace as we move into the future.

114

Artificial Intelligence for IT Operations (#AIOps) will move from early adopter to mainstream, but it will take 5 to 10 years. As AI continues to improve, #ITOps will get bigger returns. #HybridIT

115

In the near future, #AIOps discussions will focus more on automated remediation because fixing the problem is as important as finding the problem. #HybridIT

116

Analytics and automation have started helping and will continue to get better and more widespread. #HybridIT

117

Automated #AIOps will evolve to tell you, "Here's the problem and here's how to fix it; I can do that for you," for all but the most complex problems. #HybridIT

118

The push to improve automated anomaly detection and intelligent baselining (#AIOps) will increase. #HybridIT

119

Artificial intelligence will drive new types of remediation to deal with unknown issues. Have you started using AI in your IT operations? #HybridIT

120

With the number of cloud outages, hosting applications in multiple clouds will be common. However, you'll need tools that can monitor across cloud vendors. #HybridIT

121

Private and hybrid clouds are growing, so tools will have to evolve to monitor all infrastructures and show data in one place. #HybridIT

122

With the lack of SaaS transparency, #APM / #DEM will increase in importance. #HybridIT

123

With more apps moving to cloud vendors, a new metric for SLAs will appear. It will measure how fast you communicate issues to users, to force transparency. #HybridIT

124

#DevOps will increasingly push #ITOps to move faster. Automation will be a key to success. #HybridIT

125

#SecOps, #DevSecOps, and #NetSecOps are all going to impact #ITOps sooner than later. #HybridIT

126

Container discussions will move from a technology focus to a business value focus, and #HybridITmanagement is key to showing value. #HybridIT

127

Monitoring solutions will evolve into a huge encyclopedia of info to help app developers and testers understand when and where issues occur and what caused them. #HybridIT

128

Monitoring + Robotic Process Automation (#RPA) will automatically find and fix problems like a human. RPA is in its infancy now, watch it grow. #HybridIT

Share the AHA messages from this book socially by going to
http://aha.pub/HybridITOps

Section VIII

Conclusion

IT Operations teams are now seeing the benefit of having hybrid IT management solutions. To deliver the quality of service that their users are expecting and to move faster than their competitors, they need the help of hybrid IT solutions.

With better monitoring, reporting, use of artificial intelligence, and automation tools, businesses can manage the ever-increasing complexity of IT and improve service quality.

129

Hybrid IT management requires people, processes, and technology. The technology and tools make advancement possible and the processes help provide consistent service, but people are the innovators. #HybridIT

130

#HybridITmanagement solutions give you a handle on how many of your services are being consumed by your customers and whether they're performing adequately. #HybridIT

131

How many screens do you need to sit in front of and glance at before you understand where your service levels are? #HybridIT

132

#HybridITmanagement solutions let you know how many users you have and if they are satisfied. #HybridIT

133

#HybridITmanagement solutions monitor everything in your business to help you understand how situations arise and which are impacting the business the most, so you can then remediate. #HybridIT

134

#HybridITmanagement solutions help you understand your IT and business operations better. #HybridIT

135

Measure your cloud and other vendors on their capacity to serve you. If you don't, you're flying blind. #HybridIT

136

#HybridITmanagement solutions help ensure new applications are being deployed with respect to corporate policies. #HybridIT

137

#HybridITmanagement solutions help you set best practices that your operators can use to activate, and execute automatically, to solve issues. What are your best practices? #HybridIT

138

#HybridITmanagement solutions give people access to all the data you have in one place so it's easier for you to let people analyze to fit their needs. #HybridIT

139

#HybridITmanagement is not just about purchasing a software package to achieve certain objectives, it's about finding specialists who are innovative and can help you bring your business to the next level. #HybridIT

140

Impose your business value dashboards on your providers so they see how their service delivery is impacting your KPIs. #HybridIT

About the Authors

Ian Bromehead
Director of Product Marketing, Micro Focus
IT Operations Management

A thirty-five-year veteran in the industry, Ian Bromehead joined Hewlett Packard in 1986 and spent seventeen years in HP Consulting, where he delivered consulting services to large French accounts.

Ian has successfully delivered outcomes in enterprise architecture, ITSM/ITOM solution architecture, and IT Transformation projects. He held roles in the USA and Europe in business and partner development and technical alliances prior to his present position in global product marketing.

In his current role, Ian has led programs that have resulted in consistent double-digit growth over the last eight years of the Operations Bridge business within the Micro Focus ITOM portfolio.

Ian graduated with an honors degree at Sheffield University before he joined a small start-up focusing on industrial software development. He then moved to take responsibility of software development teams and international projects in France, tripling the team's productivity in two years.

Ian lives near Lyon, France, where he enjoys restoring his old Triumph car, riding his motorbike, country walking, and listening to music.

Wes Cooper
Senior Product Marketing Manager, Micro Focus
IT Operations Management

Wes Cooper has spent much of his career with Hewlett Packard Enterprise and Micro Focus, holding roles across multiple business units, including business development, sales, enablement, and product marketing. Today, he works in supporting the development and delivery of Go-To-Market strategies for the Operations Bridge. Wes lives in Dallas, Texas, with his family and enjoys traveling, kayaking, and participating in running events.

Michael Procopio
Senior Product Marketing Manager, Micro Focus
IT Operations Management

Michael Procopio is an author, keynote speaker, technologist, and marketer with twenty-five years of experience in pre-IPO and Fortune 500 high-tech organizations as a business leader and technology and marketing manager. He also has fifteen years in network and systems management as a solution architect, product manager, and technical marketing manager, is the author of fourteen books, and is a speaker at numerous conferences globally.

In his current role, Michael is a senior product marketing manager working on marketing programs for the Operations Bridge business within the Micro Focus ITOM portfolio. He lives in Morro Bay, California, where he enjoys science fiction movies and books, riding his bicycle, and being a foodie.

AHAthat®

THiNKaha has created AHAthat for you to share content from this book.

- Share each AHA message socially: http://aha.pub/HybridITOps
- Share additional content: https://AHAthat.com
- Info on authoring: https://AHAthat.com/Author